The Best-Ever Book of

SHIPS

Philip Wilkinson

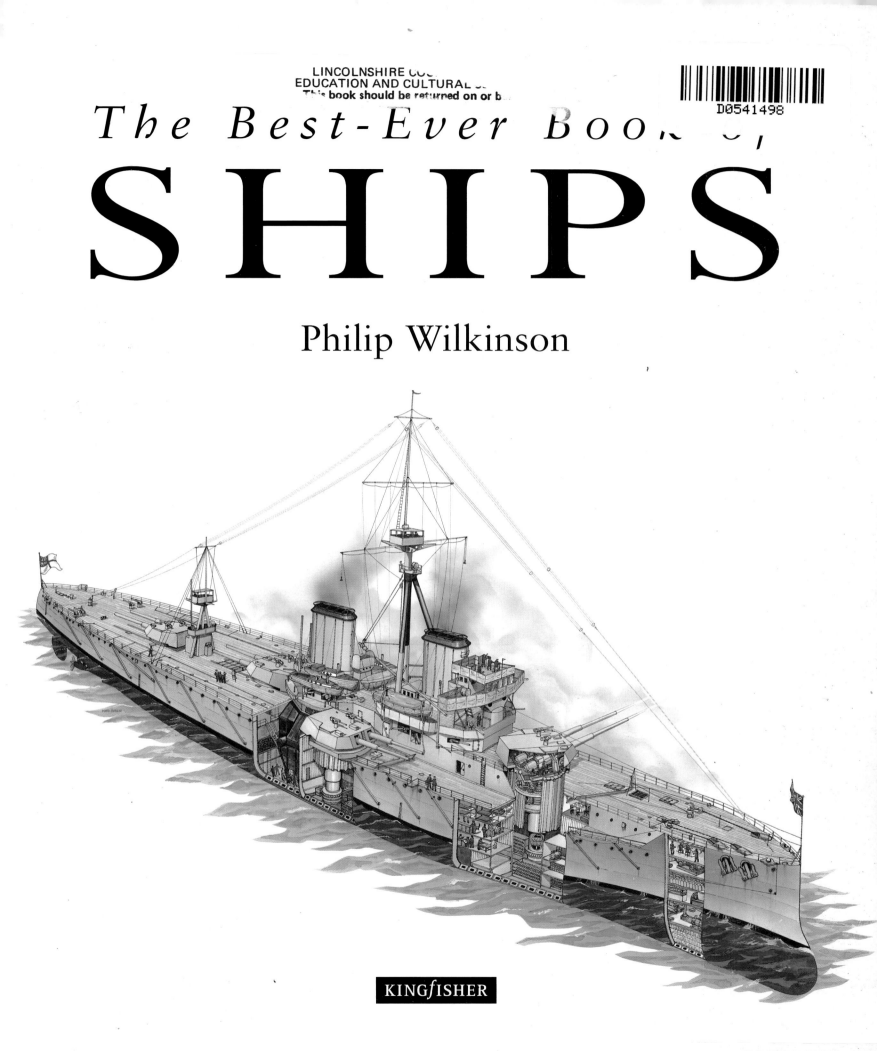

KING*fisher*

KINGFISHER
Kingfisher Publications Plc
New Penderel House,
283–288 High Holborn,
London WC1V 7HZ
www.kingfisherpub.com

First published in hardback by
Kingfisher Publications Plc 2000
First published in paperback by
Kingfisher Publications Plc 2002

10 9 8 7 6 5 4 3 2 1 (HB)
1TR/0400/SIN/MA/157MA
10 9 8 7 6 5 4 3 2 1 (PB)
1TR/0302/GC/MA(MA)/128CHST

A CIP catalogue record for this book is available
from the British Library.

ISBN 0 7534 0448 6 (HB)
ISBN 0 7534 0689 6 (PB)

Editor: Julie Ferris
Art director: Mike Davis
Consultant: Dr Peter Marsden
Production controller: Jacquie Horner
DTP co-ordinator: Nicky Studdart
Picture manager: Jane Lambert
Proofreader: Sheila Clewley
Cover illustration: David O'Connor
Indexer: Sue Lightfoot

The Publisher would like to thank the National Maritime
Museum, London, for their help and
co-operation in the production of this book.

Printed in Hong Kong

CONTENTS

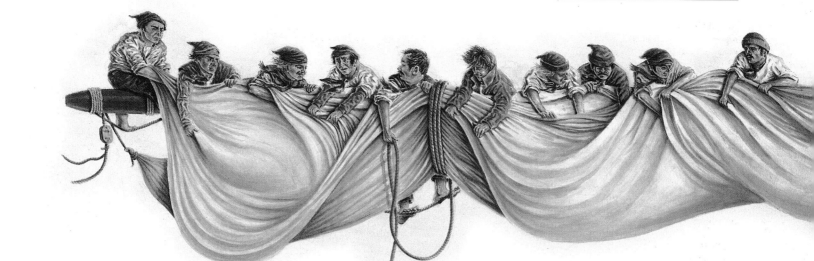

INTRODUCING SHIPS

Since the earliest times, people have sailed the seas, building a huge variety of ships for trade, to go to war and to travel across unknown oceans to new lands. Ships can be powered by oars or sails, steam or diesel engines, and can have the elegant wooden structure of a galleon or the tough steel hull of a battleship. All have fascinating stories – tales of bravery, inventiveness, and mastery of the seas.

The best ships

Some ships are successful because of their speed, like the clippers of the 19th century. Others, like Viking longships, succeed because they adapt well to harsh conditions. Many catch the eye with their beauty, while others impress with their sheer size. The best of them all, from awesome galleys and battleships to elegant clippers and men of war, combine speed, strength and seaworthiness – the ability to sail well in any conditions.

A mighty liner
The vast 80,000-tonne French ship *Normandie* was one of the fastest liners of her time. Her powerful turbo-electric engines gave her impressive speed, and she crossed the Atlantic Ocean in just four days and three hours in 1935. The tugs in New York harbour look tiny next to her massive hull.

TRADE AND DISCOVERY

From the small trading boats of the Ancient Egyptians to the huge container ships of today, merchant ships have penetrated the world's seas. For much of history, traders were also explorers. Braving cold, stormy conditions in tiny ships, they searched for better routes and new sources of goods to buy and sell.

The Ancient Egyptians' small sailing boats travelled up and down the River Nile.

The Phoenicians developed the galley, which was powered by both oars and sail.

Ancient Greek ships traded around the Mediterranean.

The Romans moved goods around their large empire in ships with two square sails.

The Vikings explored the North Atlantic in their longboats.

Chinese junks could carry tonnes of cargo in their hulls.

15th-century explorers sailed in small carracks.

East Indiamen traded between Europe and the Spice Islands.

Clippers were built for speed.

Steamships meant sailors no longer had to rely on the wind.

NORTH AMERICA

SOUTH AMERICA

EQUATOR

Silver

Tobacco

Coffee

John Cabot explored Canada

Columbus sailed in the Santa Maria

Magellan sailed around the world

Magellan 1519–1521	→
Diaz 1487–1488	→
Da Gama 1497–1499	→
Cook 1768–1779	→
Columbus 1492	→
Cabot 1497	→
Barents 1596–1597	→

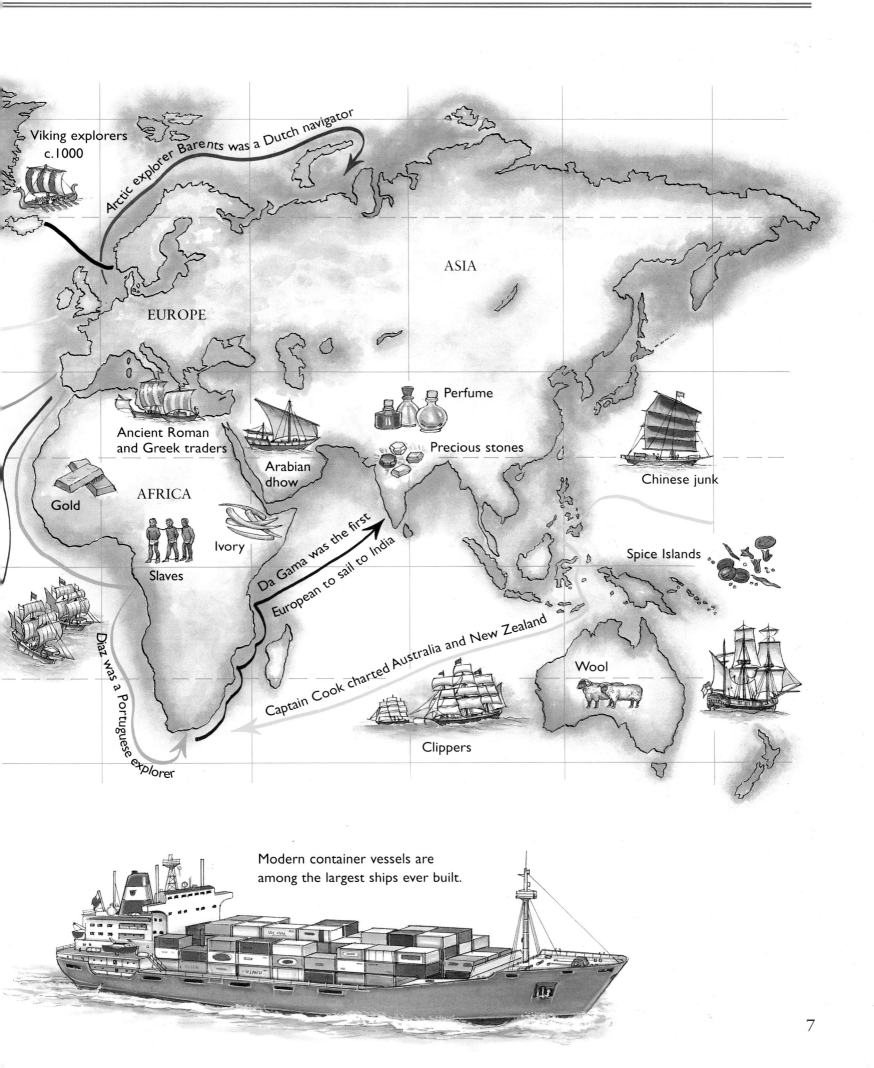

Viking explorers c.1000

Arctic explorer Barents was a Dutch navigator

ASIA

EUROPE

Ancient Roman and Greek traders

Arabian dhow

Perfume

Precious stones

Chinese junk

Gold

AFRICA

Ivory

Slaves

Da Gama was the first European to sail to India

Spice Islands

Diaz was a Portuguese explorer

Captain Cook charted Australia and New Zealand

Wool

Clippers

Modern container vessels are among the largest ships ever built.

Viking merchants

The trading vessels used by the Vikings were strong ships made of overlapping planks secured with iron nails and strengthened with cross-beams. They were broad ships, with enough room for several tonnes of cargo. The cargo was stored in the middle of the ship, and covered with animal hides to protect it from the weather. The crew stood on the small decks fore and aft to work the sail and man the rudder.

Sun compass

Viking sailors used this wooden dial to help find their way. They lined up one of the notches with a point on the horizon directly below the Sun at noon. This showed them which direction was South. The pointer was used to set the ship's course.

Rudder

Oar port

Sails were made of canvas or leather

Mainmast

Early traders

Greek trader

The sea was a vital highway in the ancient world. Early civilizations like the Phoenicians, Greeks and Vikings lived mainly along the coastline. They took to the sea to trade, sailing from one port to the next, but always keeping close to the shore. They usually ventured out into the potentially stormier waters of the Atlantic Ocean in the safer summer months only. Their trading ships were not fast, relying mainly on the wind for power, but they were compact and built for strength in dangerous northern seas.

Phoenician traders
In their homeland in Lebanon and Syria, the Phoenicians cut down high quality cedar wood to make small, sturdy ships. They traded all around the Mediterranean and the Black Sea.

Ancient Rome
The Ancient Romans used small, twin-sailed vessels for trading. These ships were usually made from pine or cypress boards, which were fixed to an oak frame with wooden pegs.

Trading far and wide
From their homes in Scandinavia, the Vikings traded all over Europe. They dealt in everything from timber and ivory to furs and glassware.

Foredeck

Ships of the East

Areas such as China and the Muslim countries of the Middle East had their own distinctive lifestyles, and developed their own forms of ships. These were often beautifully built vessels, with hulls and rigging that were very well adapted to local waters. They were also more advanced in some ways than the ships of the West. For example, the ship-builders of China were fitting stern rudders on their large, ocean-going junks around 1,000 years before the rudder appeared in the West.

Arabian dhows
Traders in the Middle East sailed dhows – sleek vessels with one or two masts. Still widely used today, dhows are rigged with lateen (triangular) sails that enable them to sail close to the wind.

Chinese junks

In the 14th and 15th centuries, the Chinese sent out expeditions to explore the Far East and the Pacific. The junks used by these Chinese navigators were large, flat-bottomed vessels with a high stern and square bow. Similar vessels still sail off the coasts of China today. The hull of a junk is very strong because it is divided by a series of cross-walls called bulkheads. The bulkheads create watertight compartments in the hull and make the ship rigid. A junk's sails, which are usually rectangular, are supported by many long strips of bamboo called battens. Smaller junks sail on China's rivers.

Navigation
Many navigation devices were invented by Arab astronomers and scientists. Sailors used the astrolabe to measure the height of the Sun at noon, so that they could work out latitude (distance from the equator).

A Chinese invention
The Chinese were the first people to use the compass. It appeared in China in the 4th century BC, about 1,500 years before the West. The compass consisted of a magnetized iron needle floating in a bowl of water.

Zheng He's expeditions
In the early 15th century, Chinese navigator Zheng He went on several voyages of conquest and exploration along China's coast. He commanded a large fleet of junks, vast vessels which dwarfed European ships of the time. However, in the 1430s, China adopted a policy of isolation and all exploration stopped.

Anchor

Bamboo batten

Sails and battens
The bamboo battens which support a junk's sails have several advantages. They stiffen the sail, allow it to be taken down quickly, and provide a useful ladder for sailors to climb aloft.

Rectangular sail made of thin cloth

Crew's quarters

15th-century European caravel

Pens for animals captured on voyages

Zheng He once brought a giraffe back from a voyage

Watertight bulkhead

11

Voyages of discovery

During the 15th and 16th centuries, explorers set out from Spain and Portugal in search of the best route to Asia. They wanted to reach the Spice Islands (Indonesia), to bring back the rare, valuable spices that grew there, such as pepper, nutmeg and cloves. A number of these explorers were employed by Prince Henry of Portugal, who became known as Henry the Navigator. They travelled in tiny ships, risking their lives in unknown waters in the hope of making their fortunes. Those who succeeded discovered places, such as America and parts of Africa, that were unknown to Europeans at the time.

Caravels
Many of the early Portuguese explorers favoured small ships called caravels. These lightweight vessels had crews of about 25 men and were ideal in coastal waters. They had lateen sails, which could take advantage of side winds.

Christopher Columbus
Christopher Columbus was born in Genoa, Italy, but his journeys were financed by the Spanish royal family. His four voyages to the West Indies opened up routes across the Atlantic Ocean.

First around the world
In 1519, Ferdinand Magellan set off from Portugal with five ships and 260 men. During the voyage, most of the crew, including Magellan, died and four ships were lost. But, in 1522, 18 men returned home, having travelled all the way around the world.

The New World
Columbus hoped to reach the Spice Islands by sailing westwards across the Atlantic, rather than following the eastward route of the Portuguese explorers. At this time, no-one knew about the existence of America, so when Columbus discovered some new islands, he thought he had reached the East Indies. In fact, he had arrived in the Caribbean, and stumbled on a 'new' world. On later voyages he sailed along the coast of Central America, and visited Trinidad and many of the Caribbean islands.

Bowsprit

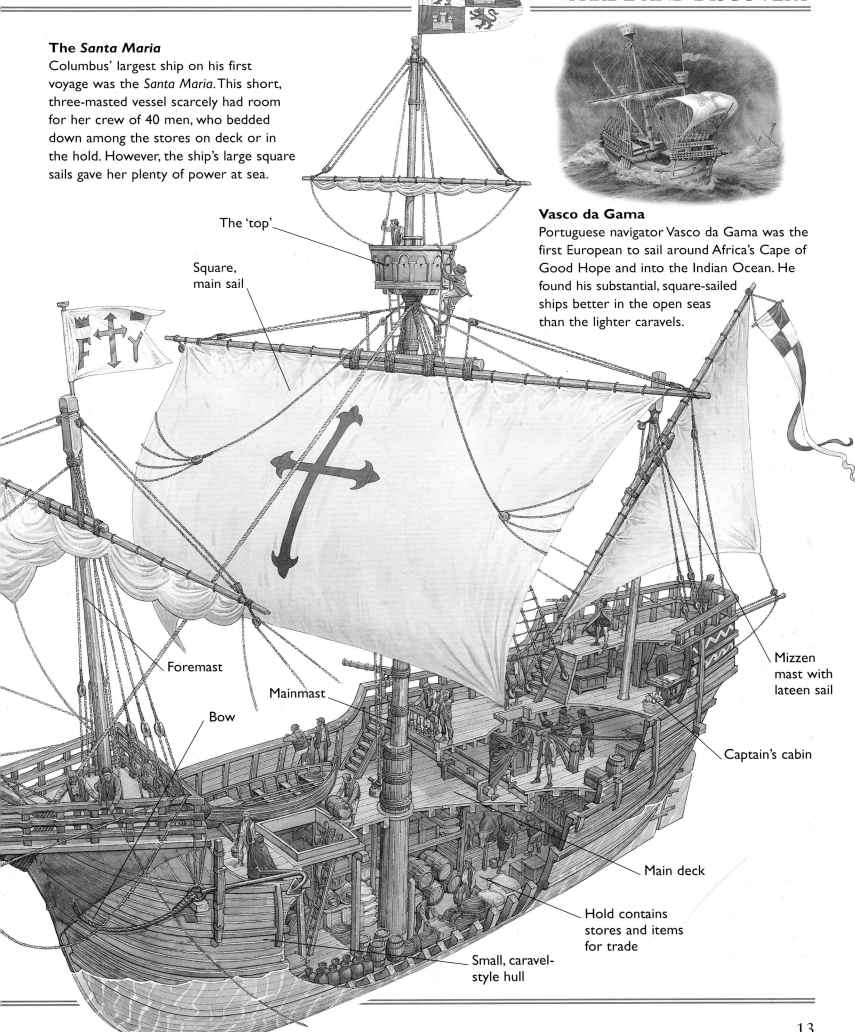

The *Santa Maria*
Columbus' largest ship on his first voyage was the *Santa Maria*. This short, three-masted vessel scarcely had room for her crew of 40 men, who bedded down among the stores on deck or in the hold. However, the ship's large square sails gave her plenty of power at sea.

Vasco da Gama
Portuguese navigator Vasco da Gama was the first European to sail around Africa's Cape of Good Hope and into the Indian Ocean. He found his substantial, square-sailed ships better in the open seas than the lighter caravels.

The 'top'

Square, main sail

Foremast

Mainmast

Bow

Mizzen mast with lateen sail

Captain's cabin

Main deck

Hold contains stores and items for trade

Small, caravel-style hull

Mapping the world

When northern Europe saw the riches that the Spanish and Portuguese were bringing back from the Spice Islands, they too wanted a share of the wealth. The southern routes to Asia were long and dangerous, so countries such as England, France and the Netherlands sent navigators to find shorter, northern routes. Some tried to sail north of North America (the 'Northwest Passage'), others went north of Russia (the 'Northeast Passage'). The routes were too icy, but both led explorers into new waters, from Canada to Lapland.

Early mapping
Navigators recorded the coastlines and ports they visited so that they could make maps. Gradually, more and more parts of the world were mapped, with Australia and America the last land masses to be shown in detail.

Latitude
Sailors used the cross-staff to work out their latitude (distance from the equator). The simple wooden instrument worked by measuring the height of a star in the sky.

The explorers of northern Europe

The search for new routes to the Far East sent British, French and Dutch explorers deep into the icy waters of the north Atlantic Ocean and the Norwegian Sea. Their ships were small and were often based on the carrack – a warship with a mixture of lateen and square sails. In spite of the skill of the sailors, many of these ships were lost in the rough northern seas. A sailor's life was filled with dangers and was often short! The ships which survived found no new route to the Far East, but they explored the little known waters of the north Atlantic, the lakes and rivers of Canada, and the seas around Greenland, Iceland and Norway.

Navigation

The first explorers found their way by sailing along the coast, keeping land in view. When they sailed out to sea, they needed instruments to help work out their position. The most important were the compass and a number of devices used to calculate latitude.

Willem Barents

Dutch explorer Willem Barents made several journeys in the 1590s in search of a Northeast Passage to the Indies. He sailed north up the coast of Norway, and explored the waters north of Lapland, which were later renamed the Barents Sea.

All round the world

British seaman Francis Drake sailed around the world in 1577–1580. Of his fleet of five ships, only the flagship, the 100-tonne *Golden Hind*, completed the voyage.

Jacques Cartier

This French explorer tried to find the Northwest Passage. He sailed up the St Lawrence River to Hochelaga (modern-day Montreal, Canada) and explored the waters around Newfoundland.

Compass

Invented in China, the magnetic compass appeared in Europe in c.1200. Sailors quickly started to use it to find their direction, even though early compasses were not always accurate.

Jolly Roger

The first pirate flags were red in colour. It is thought that the French words *joli rouge* (pretty red) became the English term 'Jolly Roger'. Each pirate band had its own flag which bore a variety of symbols such as a skeleton, skull and swords, or a skull and crossbones. Sailors quickly learned to recognize, and fear, them all.

Piracy on the high seas

For as long as ships have sailed the seas, there have been pirates – people who rob and plunder them for their cargoes. Pirates always use speedy craft – galleys with both sails and oars, four-masted galleons for raiding out at sea, or swift, sleek sloops with triangular sails for coastal waters. Pirates not only had to be fearsome, they had to be skilled sailors, constantly adjusting the ships' rigging to get the best speed.

Barbary corsairs

Muslim pirates from the North African (or 'Barbary') coast were known as 'Barbary corsairs'. They travelled in slim, fast galleys powered by both sails and oars, allowing a sudden attack and a quick getaway.

Pieces-of-eight

Spanish adventurers took gold and silver from the Americas and made it into coins called doubloons and pieces-of-eight. Pirates prized these coins – one gold doubloon was worth almost two months' of a sailor's pay.

Caribbean pirates

Piracy was common in the Caribbean Sea in the 17th and 18th centuries. The pirates began as buccaneers, defending their islands from marauding Spanish ships. But they later took to the seas as robbers, attacking any ship that promised rich booty.

Blackbeard

The most famous of the Caribbean pirates was Blackbeard. He struck terror into his victims with his cruelty. When the British navy finally caught and killed him, they hung his head from the bowsprit of their ship.

The pirate and his plunder

Pirates sailed under any flag they could lay their hands on. Unrecognized by their victims, they would come close to a ship before hoisting the Jolly Roger in the hope of scaring its crew into surrender. Then they would board and take their plunder, killing anyone who got in their way. Favourite targets in the 17th century were Spanish ships returning from the Americas loaded with treasure. East Indiamen (trade ships that travelled from the Far East to Europe), and merchant vessels in the Mediterranean and China Seas were also popular prizes.

Modern pirates

In spite of the efforts of coastguards, pirates are still active in some parts of the world. Piracy often increases at times of political unrest and war.

Science on the seas

Line of latitude

Line of longitude

Longitude
The lines of longitude are great circles around the Earth, crossing at the North and South Poles.

The 18th century was an age of great advances in science. The first explorer to be interested in scientific discovery was James Cook, a British sea captain. Cook went on three voyages to the Pacific, making astronomical observations, documenting wildlife, and plotting charts as he travelled. He was the first European to sail along the east coast of Australia.

Calculating longitude

One of the biggest navigation problems facing sailors was working out their exact position at sea. From the position of the Sun they could establish their latitude, but the best way to calculate longitude involves working out the difference between the time where you are and the time at home. However, early clocks were not accurate enough. English clockmaker John Harrison set about making a special clock, called a chronometer, that could be used at sea.

The *Endeavour*
Cook sailed the *Endeavour* on his first three Pacific voyages. The ship was originally designed to carry coal, so Cook knew it would be tough and able to carry a heavy load.

Harrison's chronometer
Finished in 1760, Harrison's fourth chronometer was the size of a large pocket watch. A copy of it was tested at sea by Captain Cook and it proved to be extremely accurate. Harrison was eventually awarded a huge prize for solving the longitude problem.

Scientific work
Cook took with him on his travels an astronomer and two botanists, together with artists who recorded all the plants and animals they saw. These included many species unknown outside the Pacific.

Limes

British 'limeys'
One of Cook's more unusual discoveries was of a medical nature. Sailors on long voyages suffered from scurvy, a disease that caused puffy, painful gums and bleeding beneath the skin. Cook realised that scurvy could be prevented if the sailors ate plenty of fruit and vegetables. He gave his men sauerkraut (preserved cabbage), plus citrus fruits such as limes and lemons, and the sailors did not develop the disease. Eventually, all British sailors had a similar diet, which is why they were nicknamed 'limeys'. We now know that it is the vitamin C in these foods that prevents scurvy.

Captain Cook
James Cook went to sea as a boy, and rose through the ranks of the navy, gaining his first command at the age of 31. He did important survey work along the coasts of North America before his Pacific journeys. Cook tried to keep on good terms with the people he met on his journeys, but was killed in a fight with islanders in Hawaii in 1779.

The *Beagle*

In 1832, British scientist Charles Darwin joined the *Beagle* as the ship's naturalist on a voyage to South America. The ten-gun brig was virtually rebuilt for the journey, but was still very small. Darwin packed his quarters with the specimens he collected – material he would use in his ground-breaking book, *The Origin of Species*.

Ships for science

After the pioneering voyages of Captain Cook, many scientists took to the seas. Men like Charles Darwin collected specimens that provided clues for major scientific theories. Then they realised that they knew little about the sea itself. In 1872, they began to put this right. The *Challenger*, the first ship fitted out for ocean research, sailed around the world, collecting data about the sea and its wildlife. The science of oceanography was born.

The *Fram*

In the 19th century, Norwegian scientist and explorer Fridtjof Nansen had the *Fram* specially designed for Arctic exploration. The *Fram*'s hull was strengthened so that, if the ice pressed against her sides, she rose up rather than be crushed by the pressure.

Deep-sea explorer
Modern undersea explorers need a research ship fitted with laboratories, accommodation for a team of scientists, space for all their supplies on a long voyage, and a vessel that can dive deep beneath the surface. Oceanographic vessels can therefore be quite large, although the actual explorer craft needs to be small and easily manoeuvrable.

Alvin

Research ship

The *Alvin*
The deep-sea vessel *Alvin* can carry people to 4,000 metres below sea level. It is easy to manoeuvre, enabling explorers to discover previously unknown creatures hiding among the rocks.

Mysteries of the deep

People have always been fascinated by the depths of the sea. But until the 20th century, the high pressures, dark and cold stopped people deep-sea diving. In 1934, American inventor Charles William Beebe built the bathysphere, a hollow steel ball lowered on a chain from a ship. In it Beebe explored to depths of 900 metres in the Atlantic Ocean. Stronger vessels were needed to explore deeper beneath the ocean, like the bathyscaphes (deep boats) and specially built submarines with strengthened hulls, such as the *Alvin*.

The *Trieste*
The *Trieste* was one of the first bathyscaphes. Her heavily reinforced hull was designed to withstand massive pressures at the bottom of the sea. *Trieste* was the first vessel to explore the Marianas Trench, the deepest part of the Pacific.

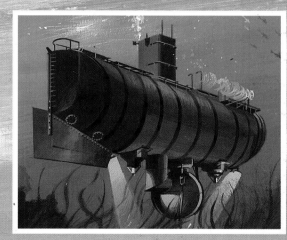

Clipper ships

With their long, slim hulls and large, billowing sails, the clippers of the 19th century were among the most elegant ships of all. Their vast area of sail meant that they were fast in a good wind, but could also keep moving in calm conditions. The first clippers were built in America. Clippers were quite compact ships, but worked in areas where speed was more important than size, such as carrying valuable cargoes across the oceans. One of the most important cargoes was tea, which they carried from China, across the Indian and Atlantic oceans, to Europe.

Sailors at work

Clippers needed a large crew to adjust the sails as the wind changed. Often, this could be done from deck, but sometimes sailors had to scramble up the rigging, clinging on to soaking, slippery sails to secure the canvas to the yard (beam).

Gold rush

In 1847, gold was discovered in California. Many people rushed to America's west coast on board the clippers to seek their fortunes. Sailors often jumped ship in California, so clippers had to take on extra crew for the onward trip to China.

Leisure time

Sailors filled in time between sleep and work with craft activities. The art of carving whalebone, called scrimshaw, was popular, especially on ships involved in whaling. Other sailors made ship models or did ropework.

In the harbour
This late-19th century photograph shows both clippers and steamships unloading their cargoes at New York's South Street Docks. By this time, most clippers had lightweight iron hulls, allowing them to carry heavier cargo.

New ships, new cargoes

Clippers ruled the seas for 20 years before steamships started to take over their trade. In 1869, the Suez Canal opened, giving the big steamers another advantage over the small tea clippers. It enabled ships to pass directly from the Mediterranean Sea to the Gulf of Suez instead of sailing all around Africa, making speed less of an advantage. But there was still a role for larger clippers, bringing bulkier cargoes such as wool and grain from Australia to England. Some of these later ships were four times bigger than the first tea clippers, and had an extra mast.

Racing across the seas
Built for speed, ships like the *Sir Lancelot* took 85 to 90 days to sail from Melbourne, Australia, to London, England, making them the swiftest vessels of their day.

World trade today

The world's largest ships are cargo carriers, and the largest ships of all are oil tankers. These massive ships can weigh up to 500,000 tonnes when fully loaded. However, the latest computerized control and navigation systems mean that they are able to sail with only a handful of crew. Other types of cargo are carried by ships built to take metal containers. With their vast hulls and decks, many modern container ships have room for more than 6,000 containers.

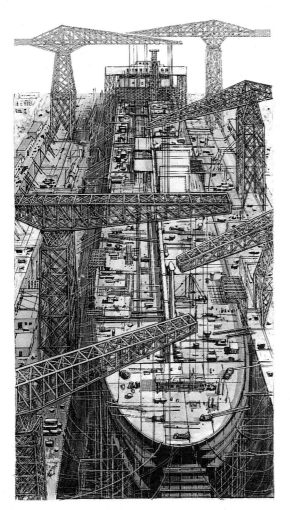

Shipbuilding
Building a modern cargo ship is a huge project needing a large workforce and massive investment. Only a few of the world's shipyards have facilities big enough to build these monsters of the seas. Japan is the world's leading shipbuilding country.

Containers
The containers loaded on to container ships come in two standard sizes, one exactly twice the size of the other.

In port
Modern cargo ships are built to take large numbers of containers. These metal boxes are built to a standard size so that they can be stacked together safely. In port, a specially designed crane removes the containers one by one, and loads them on to waiting trains or lorries. A large modern port, such as Singapore or Rotterdam in Holland, may have many quays and cranes, so that dozens of ships can be loaded and unloaded at once.

Pollution
When an oil tanker is involved in an accident, oil can spread for kilometres in a thin 'slick' on the surface of the sea. Damage to wildlife and beaches can take years to put right.

Trade on the seas
Modern container ships are ideal for transporting vast quantities of heavy cargo around the world. The world's large ports are built to be fully 'container-friendly'. They have large enough docks and cranes for the long-haul container ships, and are at key points on the main long-distance trade routes. Containers may be unloaded from the long-haul vessels on to smaller, 'feeder' ships for a shorter sea journey before finally being transferred to trains or lorries.

On the bridge
The captain has a good view of the sea and is aided by the latest navigational instruments. He or she will still need the services of a pilot, a seaman with local knowledge, to help guide the vessel safely into port.

On shore
Lorries and railway rolling stock are built to standard sizes so that they can take containers from any ship that docks.

SHIPS OF WAR

From the earliest times, people have used ships in war. While early navies used their ships as troop carriers, or as giant battering rams, modern warships carry sophisticated weapons, designed to fight enemies, either on sea or in the air, from a great distance.

Salamis 480 BC
Triremes, oar-powered warships from Greece, defeated a much larger fleet from Persia in this major battle, which stopped the Persians invading Greece.

Aegospotami 405 BC
In a surprise attack off Thrace (north-west Turkey), the Spartans defeated Athens, capturing 170 Athenian ships, during the Peloponnesian war.

Lepanto 1571
In the last great galley battle, the powerful Turkish navy was crushed by a large fleet formed by an alliance of Rome, Venice and Spain.

Spanish Armada
In 1588, Philip II of Spain sent his fleet of sailing ships to try to invade England. They were defeated by the English navy and the stormy weather.

Battle of Trafalgar
In 1805, British men of war, commanded by Admiral Nelson, defeated the ships of France and Spain, foiling French emperor Napoleon's plans to invade England.

Constitution vs Guerrière 1812–14
United States' ship *Constitution* was one of six well-armed 'heavy frigates' that fought the British. Her guns were too powerful for the *Guerrière*.

Monitor vs Merrimack 1862
The American Civil War saw the first battle between ironclad warships. War at sea would never be the same again after this struggle.

Tsushima 1905
In a decisive battle of the war between Russia and Japan, Japanese cruisers and destroyers sunk 12 of their opponent's ships and captured four more.

Jutland 1916
The fleets of Germany and Britain clashed in this key battle of World War I. Both sides lost many ships, and as a result the Germans turned to submarine warfare.

Midway 1942
In this turning point on the Pacific front of World War II, the United States navy sank four Japanese aircraft carriers, but lost only one carrier of their own.

Galleys
Ancient Greeks and Romans used these oar- or sail-powered ships, the swiftest of their time. A huge ram on the front could pierce the hull of an enemy ship.

Early battleships
Warships like Henry VIII's *Mary Rose* carried guns to hole enemy craft. They were also designed to get up close to enemy ships so the crew could board them.

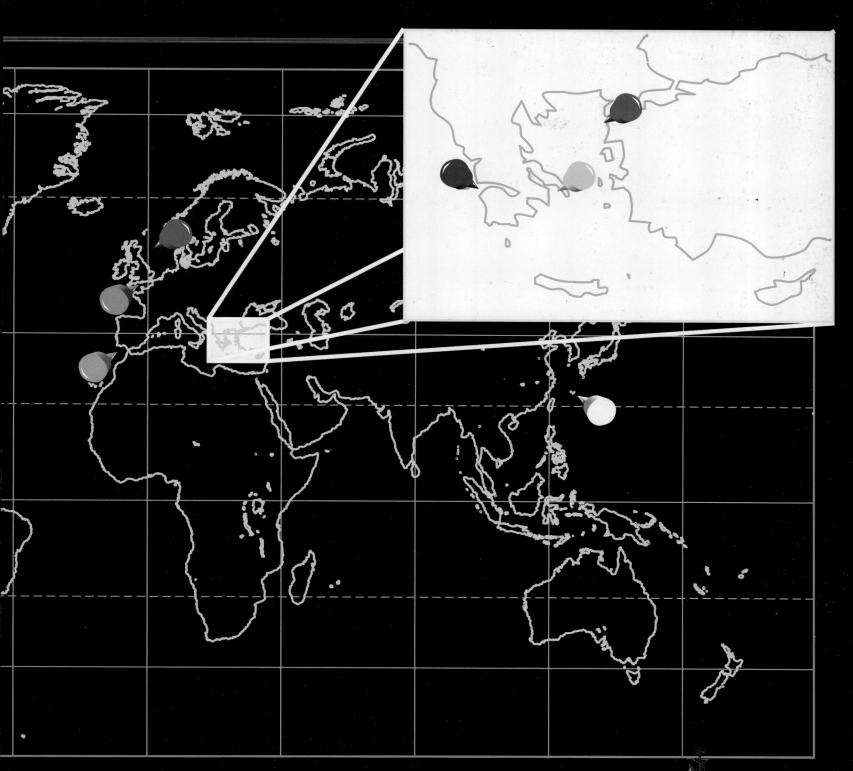

Men of war
In the 18th century, warships were built with a large area of sail. They had rows of guns on several decks, which could be fired together in a broadside attack.

Ironclads
Iron warships first appeared in North America in the 19th century. They were powered by steam engines, so navies no longer had to rely on the wind.

Dreadnought
Fast, manoeuvrable and well armed, British dreadnoughts changed the face of warships at the start of the 20th century. Soon other nations were building similar vessels.

Aircraft carriers
These large floating runways can take military aircraft near to the field of battle. These huge, expensive fighting ships can play a decisive role in a war.

Early warships

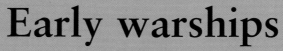

The Ancient Greeks and Romans sailed into battle on board galleys – long ships which carried both sails and oars. The oars were important because they gave the ship extra power, whatever the strength of the wind. This provided good speed and the ability to attack an enemy vessel, using the great ram on the prow to make a hole in her side. The Greeks and Phoenicians developed biremes, with two rows of oars on each side, which gave plenty of power despite a lightweight hull.

The Phoenicians
A seafaring people from the eastern Mediterranean, the Phoenicians sailed biremes. These ships had a large ram, and a single mast with a square sail.

Triremes

The Greeks wanted to make bigger, more powerful ships. But if they added extra oarsmen, the ship would have needed a longer hull, and this would have reduced its speed. They developed the trireme, a ship with three banks of oars staggered one above the other so that they took up less space.

Pulling together
Early Greek warships were quite small, with fewer than 30 oars on each side. Even so, everyone had to pull at exactly the right time, so a huge drum was used to beat out a clear rhythm for the rowers.

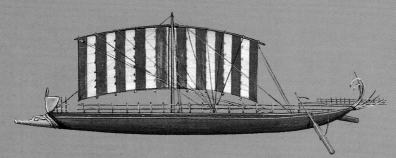

Roman warships
The Romans copied Greek designs for their warships but built them using heavier timbers, and they sometimes added an extra mast. The Romans also improved the design of boarding bridges. A Roman boarding bridge had strong hinges and a spike that pinned the bridge to the deck of an enemy ship.

Into battle

The captain of a trireme aimed first to hole an enemy ship by ramming her. As the oarsmen pulled and the ship gathered speed, the great ram crashed through the enemy's timbers. Then a wooden boarding bridge was thrown over the gap between the vessels, soldiers dashed across and hand-to-hand fighting began.

Prow rams enemy ship

Boarding plank

A naval invasion

The Bayeux Tapestry depicts the Norman invasion of England in 1066, from the crossing of the Channel to the decisive Battle of Hastings. It also shows us what Norman warships looked like.

The Normans

For hundreds of years warship technology hardly changed. The Normans of the 11th century had ships very much like those used by the Scandinavian Vikings. Their ships had large, square sails set on masts that were lowered on landing. A side rudder was used for steering, and the vessel could be rowed in calm weather.

Built for war

In medieval times (c.1000–1500), many warships, like the small, broad-beamed cogs, were simply converted cargo vessels. But soon navies were building ships especially for war. These fighting machines were still quite small ships, but had more sails, which gave them greater speed and manoeuvrability. They also had 'castles' fore and aft, and 'fighting tops' on the masts where archers could stand. In later years, they carried cannons to destroy the enemy ships.

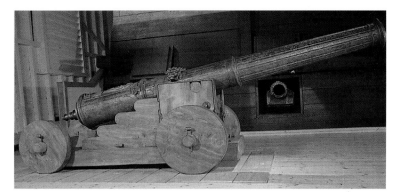

Cannon fire
The warship *Mary Rose* carried many large cannons made of bronze or wrought iron. Each front-loading gun was mounted on its own wheeled carriage, so that it could be rolled back for cleaning and loading.

The *Mary Rose*
One of English king Henry VIII's favourite ships, the *Mary Rose*, sank off the south coast of England in 1545. When archaeologists found the wreck and brought it to the surface, it told us much about the warships of the 16th century. The *Mary Rose* was built of carvel planking – instead of overlapping, the planks are laid edge to edge – on a framework of oak. The ship's four masts bore square sails.

Built for trade
Converted medieval merchant ships looked rather like Viking ships, with square sails and side rudders, but with castles fore and aft. Later examples were steered with stern rudders.

The Battle of Lepanto
In 1571, at Lepanto in the Mediterranean, the Turkish fleet fought with ships from Spain, Venice, Genoa and the Papal States in the last battle involving oar-powered galleys. Well-armed, high-sided Venetian ships played an important part in the defeat of the Turkish forces.

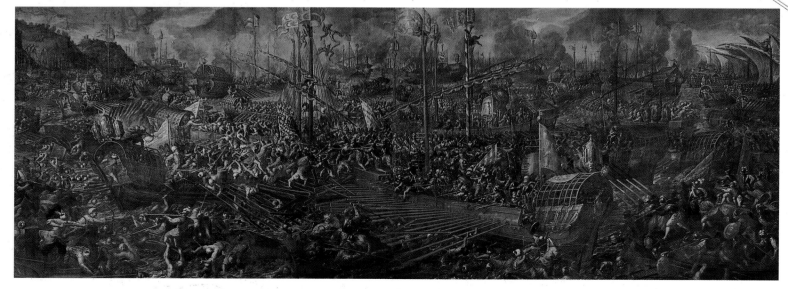

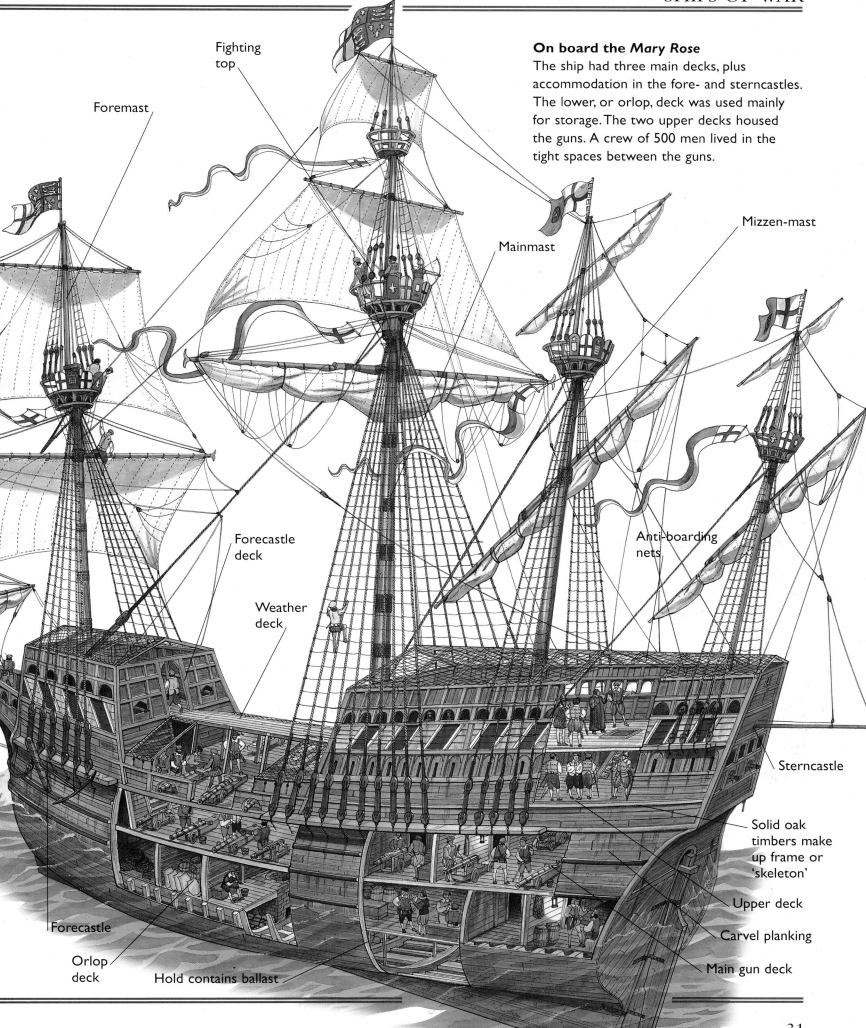

Fighting top

Foremast

Mainmast

Mizzen-mast

On board the *Mary Rose*
The ship had three main decks, plus
accommodation in the fore- and sterncastles.
The lower, or orlop, deck was used mainly
for storage. The two upper decks housed
the guns. A crew of 500 men lived in the
tight spaces between the guns.

Forecastle
deck

Weather
deck

Anti-boarding
nets

Sterncastle

Solid oak
timbers make
up frame or
'skeleton'

Upper deck

Carvel planking

Main gun deck

Forecastle

Orlop
deck

Hold contains ballast

Galleons

These large wooden fighting ships appeared on the seas during the 15th century. They were quite slender with beak-like prows, and their sides sloped inwards, making them very stable. This was important because they carried rows of large, heavy cannons. Galleons were complex and costly to build – up to 2,000 oak trees were needed for each ship. But they were worth it. Galleons ruled the seas for over 300 years. Some were even used for trade, bringing shiploads of American gold and silver to Europe.

An English galleon

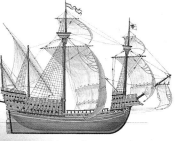
A Spanish galleon

Spanish Armada

Hoping to invade England in 1588, the king of Spain despatched a fleet, or Armada, of 151 ships. The English navy put more than 200 ships to sea in defence, and their galleons were smaller and faster than the Spanish ones. Fighting lasted on and off for ten days, with the English using cannons and burning fire-ships to damage the Armada. Finally, threatened by difficult winds and shallow waters, the Spanish withdrew.

Battling the Armada

The Spanish were used to battles in which they boarded their enemies' ships and fought hand-to-hand. But the English kept them at a distance, preventing boarding. The English also made full use of their galleons' cannons – which had a longer range than the Spanish guns – to damage their opponents' ships.

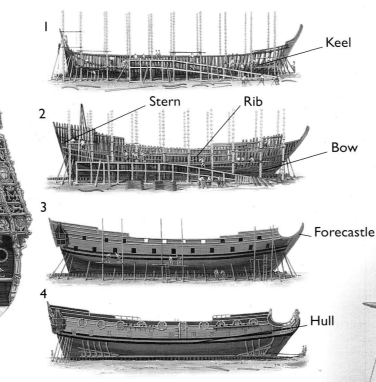

Keel

Stern   Rib

Bow

Forecastle

Hull

Building a galleon

Using the keel as the ship's 'backbone' (1), the shipbuilders added the ribs and formed the bow and stern (2). The hull was covered with planks and the decks built as construction went along (3). Next the forecastle took shape – this did not overhang like those on earlier ships, thus making the galleon more stable. Finally, the hull was waterproofed with tar (4).

The Anglo-Dutch wars

During the 17th century, the English and Dutch went to war three times over sea trade and fishing rights. The English fleet was made up of galleons that were better armed than the Dutch ships. In the first Anglo-Dutch war (1652–54), the English took advantage of their strength to gain decisive victories. The Dutch responded in the second war (1665–67) by destroying the English fleet while it was docked. The third conflict (1672–74) was more evenly matched.

Galleons at war

An English galleon has made a broadside attack on a Dutch ship, bringing down her masts and sending her crew overboard. The Dutch have fired back, but have managed only to damage their opponents' sails.

Men of war

The great wooden warships of the 18th and 19th centuries were called 'men of war'. They carried crews of up to 800 sailors on long, perilous journeys into battle. The crews had to put up with damp, cramped and dangerous conditions. They also had to be highly skilled, climbing the masts and rigging to unfurl the vast sails on the three main masts in a matter of minutes.

The press gang
Few people wanted to join the navy, so ships sent out groups of men, called press gangs, to get new recruits. If they could not persuade anyone to join, they took men by force.

Life on board
Life was hard on board a man of war. The food, ranging from salt meat to dried peas and hard biscuits, was poor quality and often rotten. Ordinary sailors had no privacy – they had to do everything from sleeping to going to the toilet in full view of everyone. But there was always plenty to do – mending and rigging the sails, scrubbing the deck or repairing the ship's planks.

Rear view
This view of the French ship *Soleil Royal* shows the stern. It contained the officers' quarters. Ship sterns were rarely attacked, so they were often ornate and had plenty of windows.

Battle formation
Enemy fleets drew together slowly at the start of a battle. Their guns were accurate only at short range, so they waited until they were close to the enemy ship before letting off a broadside (all the guns on one side firing together).

In battle
With men running everywhere in confusion, officers shouting orders, and the deafening noise of guns blasting away, a man of war could be a terrifying place during a battle. When the ship was hit by enemy fire, everyone's life was at risk. The greatest danger was from flying splinters of wood, which could be as sharp as daggers.

On the gun deck
As men loaded the guns and got ready to fire, young boys called 'powder monkeys' ran across deck with gunpowder from the magazine (store room). Then everyone stood clear, because the guns recoiled (jumped backwards) as they fired.

Battle damage
In this painting, the American ship *Constitution* has defeated the British ship *Guerrière* in the British-American War of 1812. Ship carpenters could repair damage to a hull, but could do little about the masts and rigging. Without working sails, a ship was disabled, and the enemy crew could board her.

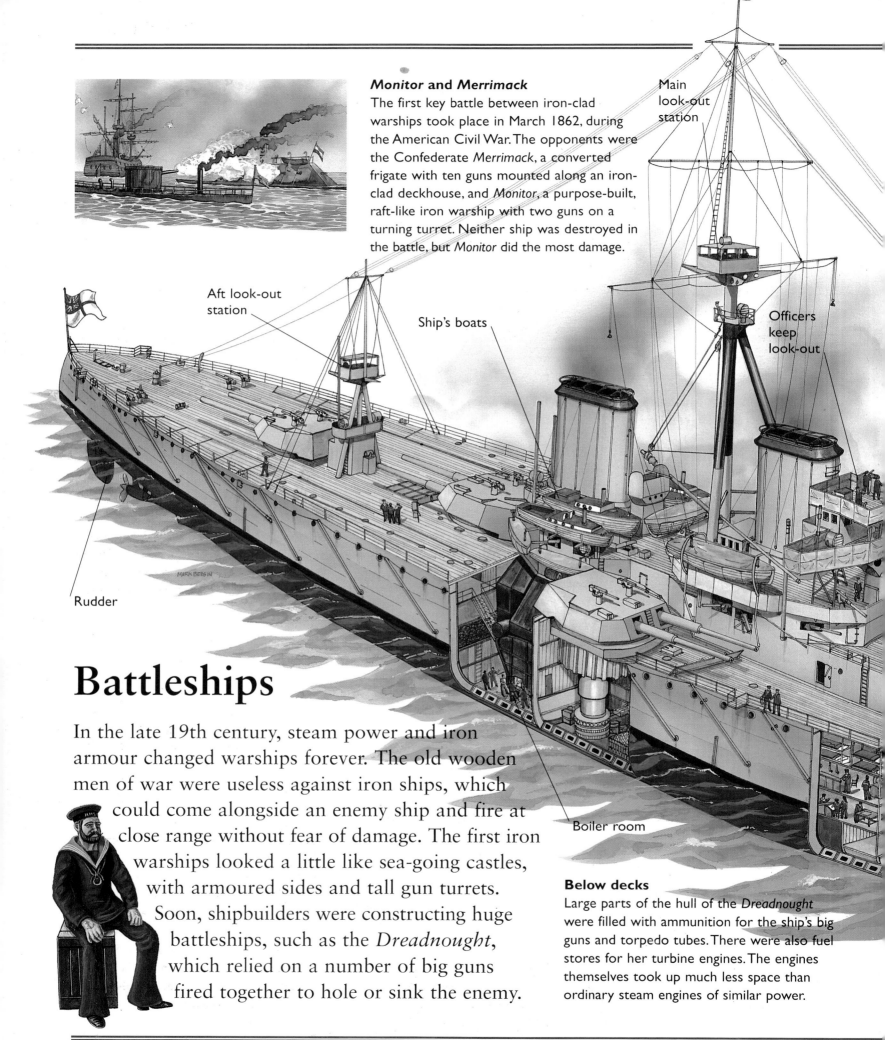

Monitor and *Merrimack*
The first key battle between iron-clad warships took place in March 1862, during the American Civil War. The opponents were the Confederate *Merrimack*, a converted frigate with ten guns mounted along an iron-clad deckhouse, and *Monitor*, a purpose-built, raft-like iron warship with two guns on a turning turret. Neither ship was destroyed in the battle, but *Monitor* did the most damage.

Main look-out station

Aft look-out station

Ship's boats

Officers keep look-out

Rudder

Boiler room

Battleships

In the late 19th century, steam power and iron armour changed warships forever. The old wooden men of war were useless against iron ships, which could come alongside an enemy ship and fire at close range without fear of damage. The first iron warships looked a little like sea-going castles, with armoured sides and tall gun turrets. Soon, shipbuilders were constructing huge battleships, such as the *Dreadnought*, which relied on a number of big guns fired together to hole or sink the enemy.

Below decks
Large parts of the hull of the *Dreadnought* were filled with ammunition for the ship's big guns and torpedo tubes. There were also fuel stores for her turbine engines. The engines themselves took up much less space than ordinary steam engines of similar power.

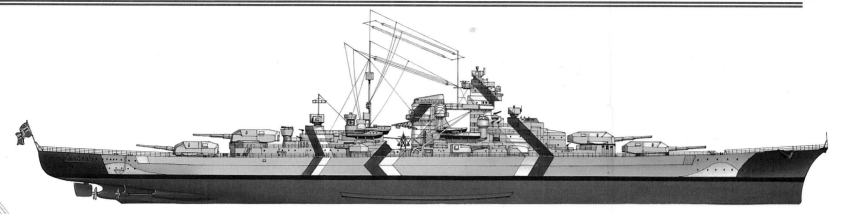

Large or small

In the 20th century, battleships got bigger and more powerful, with faster engines and larger guns. The world's navies competed with each other to build the biggest, most impressive battleships. During World War II, the Japanese developed the Yamato class of ship. Each Yamato warship weighed an amazing 74,168 tonnes, making them the largest battleships ever built. But few navies could afford such monster ships. After the war, they came to rely more on long-range missiles fired from much smaller, cheaper vessels.

The *Bismarck*

At 52,832 tonnes, the *Bismarck* was one of the largest German ships of World War II. She had a top speed of 56 kilometres an hour and large, 38-centimetre bore guns. However, this awesome ship had a short career. She was sunk by the British navy in 1941, only two years after her launch.

The *Kirov*

In the 1970s and 1980s, the Soviet Union (Russia) built several *Kirov*-class nuclear battle ships. Each of these large ships was powered by two on-board nuclear reactors. They were highly valued because they could sail for vast distances without refuelling. The vessels were scrapped in the 1990s because they were so expensive to service.

Gun turret

Officers' mess

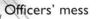

Hold contains ammunition

Dreadnought

The British ship *Dreadnought* was launched in 1906. She had ten big guns, five torpedo tubes, but no small guns at all. She was also the first battleship to be driven by steam turbines, giving a top speed of 39 kilometres an hour. This combination of speed and massive fire power impressed naval commanders. Soon there were many imitations, and all large warships in the early 20th century became known as 'dreadnoughts'.

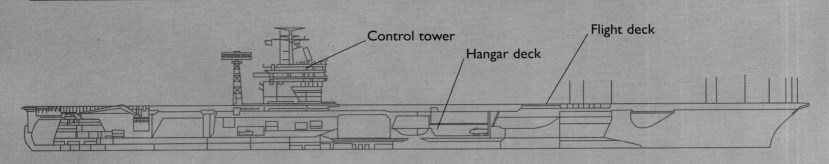

Control tower

Flight deck

Hangar deck

Battle fleet

Modern navies go into battle at long distance. Their ships can fire nuclear guided missiles that travel hundreds of kilometres to their targets. They can also use aircraft carriers to deliver fighters and other aeroplanes to the war zone. A modern battle fleet may consist of a large carrier defended by smaller ships called destroyers, or a number of smaller ships firing at long range.

Inside the aircraft carrier
Much of the space below deck on the USS *Nimitz* aircraft carrier is taken up by accommodation for some 3,000 personnel. Two pressurized, water-cooled nuclear reactors power the *Nimitz* to speeds of over 56 kilometres per hour – impressive for a vessel the height of a 25-storey building. Over 90 aircraft can be stored on the hangar deck.

USS *Enterprise*
The first nuclear-powered aircraft carrier, and the longest warship ever built, is the USS *Enterprise*. About 75 aircraft can take off from her 372-metre long flight deck. She was launched in 1961, and is still in active service.

Missile destroyer

Destroyers traditionally were small, fast-moving warships, armed with both guns and torpedoes and used for defending the main fleet and attacking submarines. Modern destroyers have guided missiles and perform a wide range of duties.

Aircraft carriers

The most impressive modern warships are aircraft carriers, massive vessels with vast flight decks from which aircraft can take off and land. The ships are so large and expensive that only major powers, such as the United States, can afford them. They have played a key role in most modern conflicts, from World War II to the Gulf War and the Balkan conflict.

An aircraft waits to take off from the flight deck of United States' carrier, *John F. Kennedy*

The flight deck

Fighter-bombers, surveillance aircraft, anti-submarine planes and helicopters can all take off from the flight deck of a modern carrier. The deck must have enough space for these aircraft to park, as well as a runway for take-off and landing. Today's warships go into attack with missiles, which have a longer range and greater accuracy than guns. Different types of missiles can be aimed at the enemy's ships or their aircraft. Hi-tech equipment in the control tower means that everything can be controlled or monitored at a distance.

Viking settlers

During the 9th and 10th centuries, the Vikings travelled far from their native Scandinavia. They founded settlements in Iceland and Greenland and, in 1001, reached the coast of Newfoundland. They were probably the first Europeans to reach America.

California gold rush

When gold was discovered in California in 1848, people rushed there, hoping to make their fortunes. Land travel across North America was hard, so many travelled to California by clipper ship around South America.

NORTH AMERICA

19th-century migration

Millions of people left Europe in the 19th century, seeking a better life in lands such as the United States and Canada.

The Pilgrims

Braving long, hard journeys in tiny, poorly equipped ships, settlers like the Pilgrims peopled the east coast of North America in the 17th century.

PEOPLING THE WORLD

Throughout history there have always been movements of people, as men and women decide to leave their homes and start a new life in a new land. Ships, whether 19th-century steamships or modern liners, have plenty of room for both people and their luggage, so they have played a huge part in these migrations.

SOUTH AMERICA

Luxury liners

In the early 20th century, people travelled on huge passenger liners. The rich had luxury cabins and the poor had more basic accommodation.

Aircraft travel
In the 1950s and 1960s, jet aircraft became widespread and air fares started to fall. Many people took advantage of this faster means of transport. The great age of sea travel was over.

EUROPE

ASIA

Refugees
When the Vietnam War ended in 1976, refugees fled the country, fearing the communist government. Many took to their boats, risking death by living on cramped, unseaworthy vessels.

Slave trade
Some European merchants grew rich taking Africans on cramped ships to America as slaves. Many of the slaves died in the appalling conditions on board the ships.

AFRICA

Steamships
In the 19th century, ships with steam engines became more reliable than sailing ships, and they were soon used for both long and short routes. Steamships were ideal wherever a regular service was needed.

COME TO AUSTRALIA

Migration to Australia
With a widespread publicity campaign, the government of Australia encouraged many people to settle in their country during the 1950s. Passenger liners offered cheap fares.

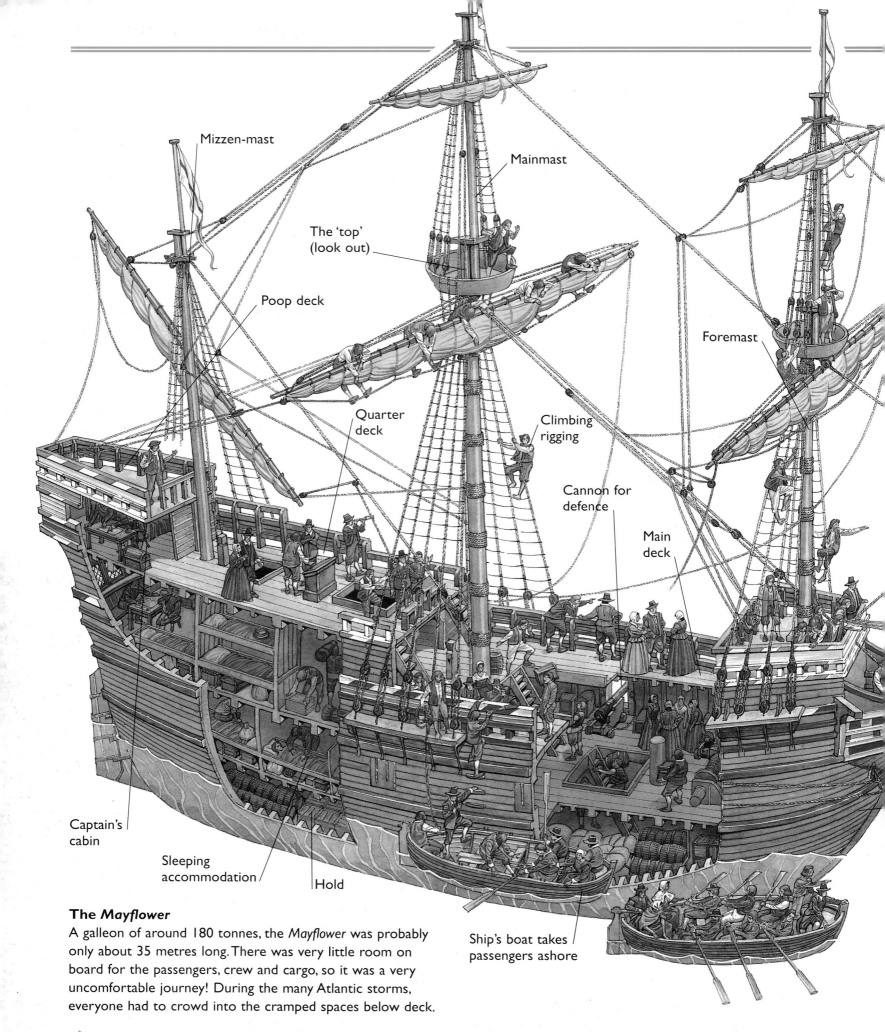

Mizzen-mast

Mainmast

The 'top'
(look out)

Poop deck

Quarter
deck

Climbing
rigging

Foremast

Cannon for
defence

Main
deck

Captain's
cabin

Sleeping
accommodation

Hold

Ship's boat takes
passengers ashore

The *Mayflower*

A galleon of around 180 tonnes, the *Mayflower* was probably
only about 35 metres long. There was very little room on
board for the passengers, crew and cargo, so it was a very
uncomfortable journey! During the many Atlantic storms,
everyone had to crowd into the cramped spaces below deck.

Early settlers

At many different times in history, from the Viking period to the 20th century, people have sailed to new homes. Their reasons range from famine to fortune-hunting. One of the most famous migrations took place in 1620, when a group of people left England to establish a settlement in North America. Many of them wanted to leave their homeland because they could not practise their religious beliefs freely in England. They called themselves Pilgrims.

Thanksgiving
The Pilgrims celebrated their first year in America, and their first harvest, with a special meal. They invited members of the local Wampanoag tribe to the feast.

The Pilgrim settlers
The Pilgrims' ship, the *Mayflower*, was already old when she left Plymouth, England. But she was sturdy enough to withstand a battering from many gales during the 66-day journey across the Atlantic. She carried 102 passengers and a crew of over 40. One passenger died during the journey, but two more were born so they landed with one more passenger than they started out with.

Spritsail

Bowsprit

The landing
After arriving at Cape Cod, New England, the Pilgrims spent some weeks looking for a place to settle. They called the chosen spot Plymouth, and began to build houses there on Christmas Day in 1620.

Beakhead (about six metres long)

Wooden planks laid over oak frames

The slave trade

Between the 17th and 19th centuries, millions of Africans were forcibly transported across the seas and sold as slaves. Three continents were involved in this shameful trade. Ships left Europe with trade goods which were sold on the African coast. The ruthless captains took on a cargo of Africans, sailed to America, and sold them as slaves to plantation owners and wealthy merchants, before returning to Europe loaded with sugar or other produce. Not only did slaves have to endure appalling conditions on the ships, but they were also taken from their homes forever.

Capturing slaves

People taken as slaves were rounded up in gangs and marched to the coast. Here they were kept in pens called barracoons until an America-bound ship was ready for loading. As they boarded the ships, the slaves were held in leg-irons, with their hands tied behind their backs.

Slave ships

Most slave ships were quite small vessels of a few hundred tonnes, originally designed to carry cargo. The Africans who were forced to travel on these vessels were treated like cargo, packed together tightly on the ships' small decks.

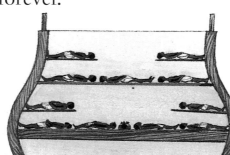

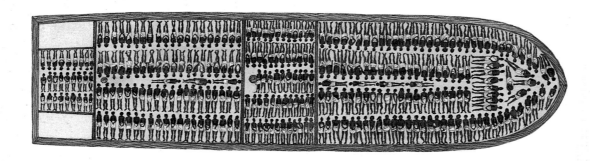

The sailors

Sailors on board a slave ship had little choice but to go along with the cruelty dealt out to the slaves. They too would have been punished had they shown any mercy. As well as maintaining discipline, they had to guard the slaves closely in case they tried to escape. Occasionally slaves tried to jump overboard, so captains often hung nets along the sides of the ships.

Life as a slave

Many slaves worked on plantations growing cotton or tobacco in the southern states of America, and on sugar plantations in the Caribbean. They had no legal rights, and were seen by their owners as property.

Meal time

Ship owners gave slaves as little food as possible on the journey. Most slaves arrived on the other side of the Atlantic thin, weak and sick.

The journey

There was no space to move on a slave ship – people were crammed into every corner. The slaves also had to endure unsanitary conditions and a very poor diet. Disease spread quickly, and as many as 15 per cent of the captives died during the journey. Others were maimed by the leg-irons and metal collars they had to wear, or were injured by being forced to lie on the deck planking throughout the journey. All were terrified because they were leaving their homes behind to live in an unknown world.

Sail to steam

Until the 19th century, sea travel was very slow and uncomfortable, deterring people from travelling overseas. The Industrial Revolution brought about the introduction of steam-powered factories in Britain, and opened up the possibility that steam engines could also be used at sea. This meant that ships would no longer have to rely on winds to power their sails. Steamships allowed shipping companies to offer passengers a regular, reliable service. They were also used to transport cargo and carry overseas mail.

A great ship-builder
The British engineer Isambard Kingdom Brunel worked on railways and bridges before building his first steamship, the *Great Western*, in 1836–1837. This large, wooden paddle steamer was used for Atlantic crossings. She was followed by the *Great Britain* and the huge *Great Eastern*, a 211-metre steamer that could carry 4,000 passengers.

SS Great Britain

For his second steamship, the *Great Britain*, Brunel used screw propellers instead of paddle wheels. Propellers were more reliable than paddle wheels which could be pushed out of the water in rough seas. He also built an iron hull, which was less prone to damage from the vibrations of the huge engines.

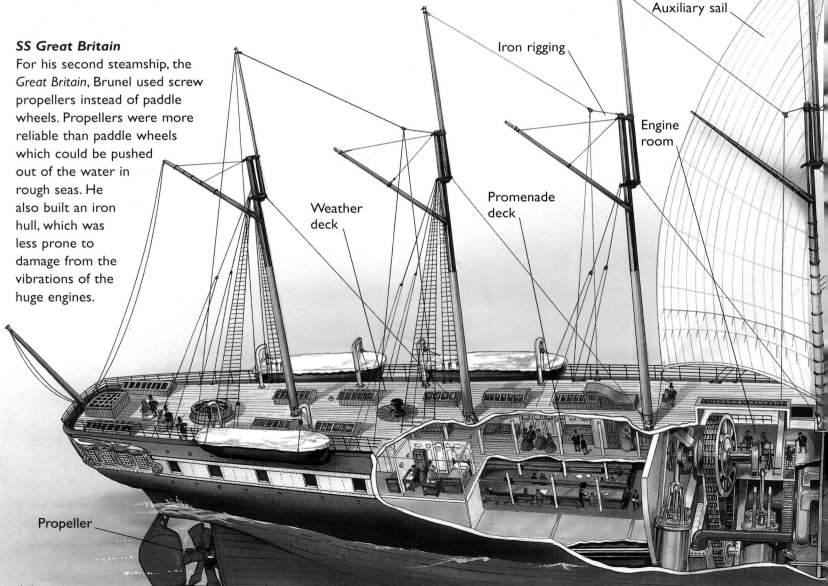

Auxiliary sail

Iron rigging

Engine room

Weather deck

Promenade deck

Propeller

Steamships

The first experimental steamships appeared at the end of the 18th century. During the next 50 years a variety of steamships developed, from Brunel's large passenger vessels to small cargo ships best suited to short journeys. Most of these ships also had sails – to save fuel when there were favourable winds, and as a source of power if the engines broke down.

Trial of strength

People argued about whether paddle wheels or propellers were more powerful. In 1845, two similar British ships, the paddle steamer *Alecto* and the propeller-driven *Rattler*, took part in a tug-of-war. *Rattler* won the contest, pulling her rival backwards at about 5 kilometres an hour.

The *Sirius*

The first ship to cross the Atlantic under steam power, the *Sirius* was a small, 700-tonne paddler. Brunel's *Great Western* began its crossing a few days after the *Sirius*, but arrived in New York just a few hours after it. The *Great Western* had travelled at a higher average speed.

Mainmast

Foremast

11.5-metre high funnel

Dining saloon

Passenger cabins

Forecastle

Emigration

During the 19th century, thousands of people left Europe, hoping for a better life in South Africa, Brazil, Canada or the United States. They travelled across the Atlantic on huge liners, and the great shipping companies, such as Cunard and the Red Star Line, competed for the business. Most of the travellers were poor and could afford only the cheapest accommodation on board. But they put up with the overcrowded conditions because they hoped they would lead a more prosperous life when they arrived.

Life on board

Most emigrants had not been to sea before, and the trip could be a harrowing experience with cramped conditions and seasickness common. Once in port they sometimes had to wait for days on deck before being allowed to disembark. They then had to pass through immigration control where they could be sent home if they did not have the right papers or were in poor health.

On board ship
Even on luxury liners like the Cunard ship *Carpathia* the cheapest accommodation (steerage) was crowded and uncomfortable. Hundreds of emigrants were crammed into dark dormitories, getting what sleep they could on hard bunk beds.

Radio communications
Italian inventor Guglielmo Marconi was the pioneer of radio. In 1901 he sent the first radio signals across the Atlantic. Radio communications made long sea journeys safer than before.

ORIENT LINE
Via Suez Canal to
AUSTRALIA

Points of departure

In the late 19th century, liners were getting bigger as well as faster. German ship owners were among the first to realise that, with bigger ships, they could make money out of the thousands of people who wanted to emigrate. Soon ships from other north European countries were also carrying large numbers of emigrants. Later, more people from southern Europe began to make the journey.

To Australia
In the 1950s and 1960s, the Australian government encouraged immigration by paying the fares of many people who wanted to settle there. Thousands of Europeans and Asians made the trip.

A new life
Full of hope, immigrants to the United States get their first glimpse of the Statue of Liberty in New York Harbor, welcoming them to the 'land of the free'.

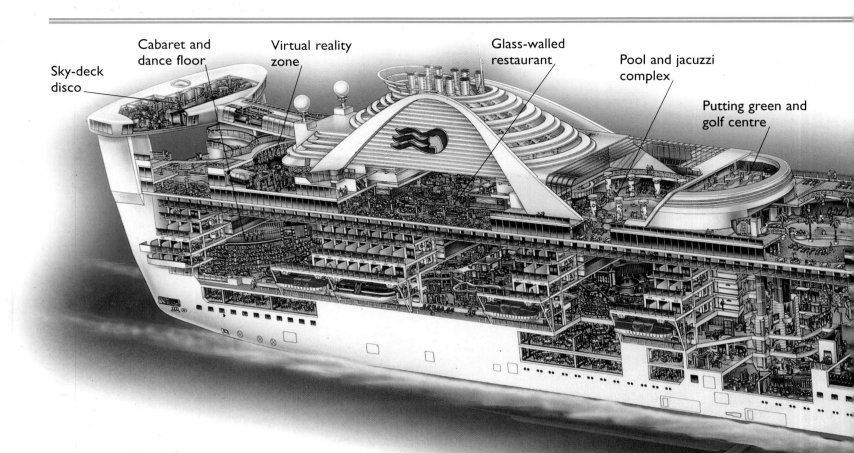

Sky-deck
disco

Cabaret and
dance floor

Virtual reality
zone

Glass-walled
restaurant

Pool and jacuzzi
complex

Putting green and
golf centre

Luxury travel

In contrast to the cramped conditions of
third class (steerage) passengers, first class
passengers on the liners of the early 20th
century travelled in great style. Today,
many people enjoy holidaying on
luxurious cruise liners, travelling from
country to country, and only going
ashore to see the sights. Packed into a
hull up to 300 metres in length, today's
liners contain cabins with every comfort,
a range of places to eat and drink, and a
variety of entertainments, from cinemas
to casinos, shops to swimming pools.
Whether cruising the Mediterranean
or crossing the Atlantic, travellers are
offered all the facilities they could
expect on shore in a top-class hotel.

A life of ease
Passengers on the liners of
the early 20th century lived
a life of great luxury, with
all their needs attended
to by a large crew.

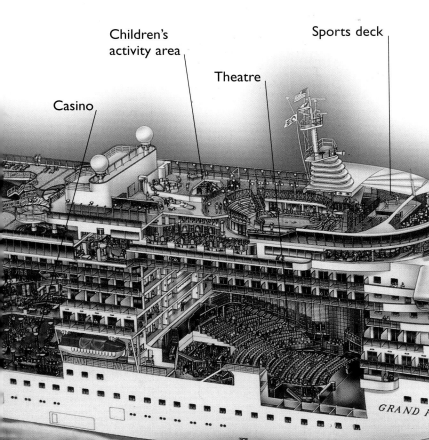

Casino

Children's activity area

Theatre

Sports deck

GRAND PRINCESS

Travel in style

The largest passenger ship in the world, the *Grand Princess*, carries 2,600 passengers on 12 decks. From the passenger staterooms and suites to the large public areas, the ship offers a combination of luxury and modern convenience. The facilities on board the *Grand Princess* include a library offering CD-ROM access, a games area with virtual reality, a swimming pool that can be protected by a moving roof, and a casino decorated with holograms.

The Blue Riband

Liners of the 19th and early 20th centuries competed for the Blue Riband, an award for the fastest Atlantic crossing. The *Pacific*, which won the award in 1851, averaged 24 kilometres an hour. But this record was soon broken. The famous liner *Mauretania* held the Riband from 1907 until 1929 and reached a top speed of 50 kilometres an hour.

Record breaker

One of the most successful liners of the 1930s was the *Normandie*. She was a large vessel, 298 metres long, and could carry about 1,975 passengers and 1,345 crew. Her hull was designed for speed, even in rough weather, and her Atlantic crossing in just under four days earned her the Blue Riband.

NORMANDIE

DISCOVERING SHIPS

Over the centuries, ships have been used in a diverse range of roles, and shipbuilding and navigation technologies have evolved dramatically. Historians and marine archaeologists look to historical documents, paintings, myths and folktales, as well as shipwrecks, to tell them about ships and life at sea in the past.

Titanic
This huge liner was said to be indestructible, but she was sunk by an iceberg in 1912 on her maiden voyage. Divers have found and studied the wreck, and salvaged objects from the ship.

Exxon Valdez
In 1989, the oil tanker *Exxon Valdez* ran aground off Alaska, spilling 50 million litres of oil and polluting thousands of kilometres of coastline.

Constitution
Some sailing ships, like the famous United States frigate *Constitution*, have been painstakingly restored by naval history experts.

Spanish Armada
Many of the Spanish ships involved in Philip II's ill-fated attempt to invade Britain in 1588 were wrecked off the coast of Ireland.

Santa Maria
In 1492, Christopher Columbus sailed to America on the *Santa Maria*, but the vessel was wrecked off the coast of the island of Hispaniola (modern Haiti).

NORTH AMERICA

SOUTH AMERICA

Medusa
Survivors of this famous 19th-century shipwreck were painted by the French artist, Géricault.

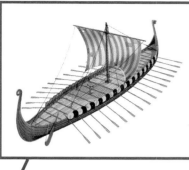

The Vikings
Although the Vikings were skilled sailors, they lost many ships in the stormy waters of the North Atlantic. Remains of their cargoes are occasionally found.

Vasa
This 17th-century Swedish royal warship was recovered from the seabed by marine archaeologists. Her finely decorated timber hull is preserved in a museum.

Mary Rose
Henry VIII's favourite battleship, the *Mary Rose*, sank in 1545. In 1982, marine archaeologists raised the ship.

ASIA

EUROPE

AFRICA

AUSTRALASIA

Chinese junks
Many of these large vessels, their holds full with rich cargoes, have been wrecked off the Chinese coast in the East and South China Seas.

Bismarck
This large German battleship of World War II was sunk during an attack by British ships and aircraft in 1941, only two years after her launch.

Orient
The French flagship *Orient* exploded at the Battle of the Nile in 1798. Wreckage was widely scattered, but divers have found items such as cutlery and glassware intact.

Myths and mysteries

The sea has always been a frightening and hazardous place. Hidden rocks or punishing weather can bring a ship down, no matter how skilled her captain and crew. Sailors have always told stories about mythical creatures and mysterious forces, tales which try to explain some of the power of the sea. Terrible monsters, gods of the winds, and beautiful but deadly mermaids are just a few of the mythical dangers lurking in the depths.

Odysseus and the sirens

In Greek legend, sirens were sea demons, half-woman and half-bird, whose beautiful song lured sailors to their deaths on the rocks. The hero Odysseus survived hearing the song. He made his crew block their ears with wax and tie him to the mast.

Flying Dutchman

Germanic myths tell of the *Flying Dutchman*, whose captain sold his soul to the Devil in exchange for a safe passage around the Cape of Good Hope. But the Dutchman made a fatal mistake. Because he did not ask to make the voyage only once, he was forced to sail back and forth forever.

Mary Celeste

The American cargo ship *Mary Celeste* left New York in November 1872, bound for Genoa, Italy. The following month she was found deserted, her sails set for stormy conditions and the ship's boat gone. The captain and crew were never seen again. They seemed to have abandoned ship in a hurry, but no-one ever found out what happened to them.

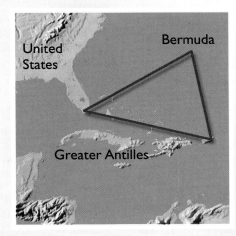

United States

Bermuda

Greater Antilles

Bermuda Triangle

Scientists are baffled by the mysterious disappearances of more than 50 ships in this part of the Atlantic Ocean, between Bermuda, the Great Antilles and the southern coast of the United States.

Sailor's lore

Alone in the middle of a great ocean, a ship can sail for days without sighting another vessel. If she has an accident, there is no-one to explain how it happened. These mysteries have inspired sailors' tales of disappearing ships and vanishing crews. Stories about crafts dogged by misfortune and mishaps have led to many superstitions. Some sailors believe that it is unlucky to begin a voyage on Friday (the day of Jesus' crucifixion), others that the colour green is unlucky, or that whistling when it is calm will bring on a storm. Having women and priests on board is also conisdered unlucky by some fishermen!

Viking prows

The wooden bows of Viking warships were carved with the heads of fearsome mythical beasts – snarling dragons, hissing snakes and terrifying bird-like creatures. They were probably intended to scare enemies and ward off evil spirits.

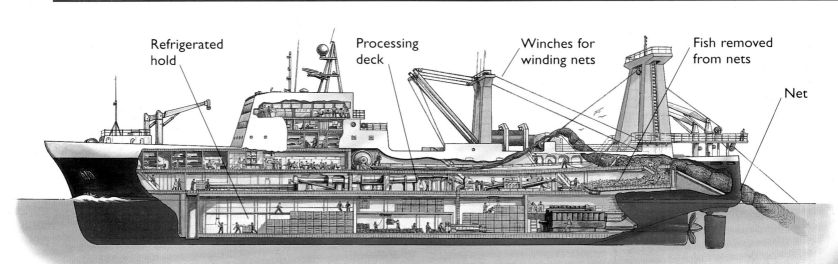

Refrigerated hold

Processing deck

Winches for winding nets

Fish removed from nets

Net

Other kinds of boats

There is a ship or a boat for virtually every job that needs to be done at sea. They range from gigantic oil tankers to ocean-going yachts, from flimsy rowing boats to lifeboats that go out in all weather to rescue those in trouble at sea. Although many of them look as if they have not changed for years, they often carry the most up-to-date technology, such as powerful computers and satellite navigation.

Factory ship

With this type of ship, fish can be caught and processed while still at sea. As the nets are wound in, the fish are removed and conveyed to a processing deck, where they are scaled, cleaned and filleted. Then they are packed into boxes, and frozen in the cold store in the hold.

Ferry crossings

Large ferry ships sail back and forth, carrying passengers and cars across many of the narrow channels of the world's seas. As well as several passenger decks, modern ferries also have car decks. When in dock, a section of the ship's bow opens to allow motor vehicles to drive on and off.

Catamarans

A catamaran is a boat with two hulls. Catamarans were developed in the Pacific islands thousands of years ago, but have only been used widely in the rest of the world for about 30 years. Having twin hulls makes the boat wide, so it is very stable and can carry large sails. The craft is also lightweight, and this combination of features makes catamarans fast and ideal for racing.

Leisure and sport

Sailing is one of the world's most popular pastimes, and involves all sorts of craft, from simple, fibre-glass dinghies to luxury yachts fitted with every imaginable comfort. Sailing developed as a sport when sailing ships ceased to be used for trade and battle. For racing, the aim is to build a boat that is light in weight, can take big sails for the greatest speed, but will handle well at sea. Racing boat designers often combine old and new materials, such as traditional woods and the latest hi-tech sail fabrics.

Salvage vessel

This Russian ship is a salvage tug that helps search for wreckage and survivors when ships have sunk or aircraft have gone down over the sea. The ship carries a magnetic detector, to locate metal debris with ease.

Computer-controlled sails

Modern tankers, like this Japanese ship, sometimes have sails as well as engines. In this experimental vessel, an on-board computer set the sails so that the ship could use wind power when the weather was favourable. The owners could sometimes save up to ten per cent of the normal fuel costs in this way.

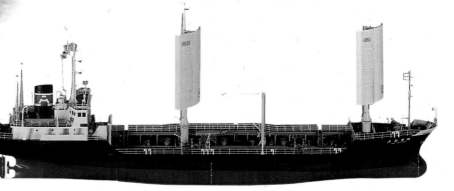

Shipwrecks

The sea is a perilous place. Even the most experienced sailors respect its natural dangers – rocks, icebergs, unpredictable currents, unexpected storms – all of which can lead to shipwreck. In times of war, ships are also in constant danger from enemy fire. The oceans and seabeds are littered with wrecks, from Ancient Roman galleys to Spanish galleons and ocean liners. Their remains are fascinating – both for what they can tell us about early ships, and for the treasure they sometimes contain.

The *Constitution*
Some historic ships have survived. The American ship *Constitution* was built in the 1790s. She was one of the fastest warships of the time. After taking part in the War of 1812 between Britain and the United States, the *Constitution* did many jobs including cargo-carrying and naval training. She was eventually restored to her original splendour.

Wreck of the *Titanic*
On her maiden voyage in 1912, the *Titanic* hit an iceberg in the Atlantic Ocean. The ice ripped a hole in the ship's hull, and she sank to the bottom of the sea, with the loss of 1,490 lives.

The *Vasa*

The wooden hull of this Swedish ship, which sank on her maiden voyage in 1628, was rediscovered in 1956. The hull and thousands of artefacts were salvaged and preserved in a special museum. The *Vasa* gives a unique insight into life on a 17th-century warship.

Finding the wreck

Salvage experts found the *Titanic* in 1985. Their cameras showed that the ship had broken into two sections, but the hull otherwise had little damage. The salvage crew used a manned submersible and remote cameras to survey the wreck, and bring fittings and other items to the surface.

The *Titanic*

The liner was built to carry 2,500 passengers in luxury — facilities included a gym, swimming pool and Turkish baths. Experts at the time believed that the ship was practically unsinkable.

Learning from shipwrecks

Old ships do not normally survive. Their hulls rot away or are taken apart for salvage. This means that much of our knowledge of ancient ships comes from pictures or early descriptions. Archaeologists are therefore fascinated by shipwrecks. A shipwreck is like a time capsule. When a ship goes down, she takes with her a complete record of life on board. Underwater conditions can preserve ship timbers and other objects that would normally rot. They can give archaeologists invaluable information about hull construction, guns, masts, cargo and the daily lives of sailors, which they would not otherwise have been able to discover.

Glossary

aft Towards the rear of the ship.

anchor A weighted structure used for mooring a vessel.

bireme An ancient warship powered by two banks of oars on each side of the hull.

bowsprit A strong wooden beam that sticks out from the front of a sailing ship, used to attach rigging for forward sails.

bridge The raised area where a ship's captain stands, steers and gives orders.

broadside Attack in which all the cannons on one side of a warship are fired at once.

bulkhead A cross-wall in the hold of a ship, often creating a watertight compartment.

caravel A light sailing ship common in the Mediterranean in the 15th and early 16th centuries.

chart A map of the sea, showing coasts, currents, islands and other features.

chronometer A highly accurate clock which keeps precise time at sea and is used to help in navigation. The first chronometer was made by English clockmaker, John Harrison.

clinker The system of building wooden ships in which the planks are overlapped.

clipper A fast ship with a large area of sail, popular for long-distance cargo carrying during the 19th century.

cog A large, medieval, square-sailed ship used for war and cargo carrying.

compass A navigation instrument that uses magnetism to find North. It was more reliable than the Sun compass.

container ship A vessel designed to carry cargo containers of a standard size.

dinghy A small, open boat.

Dreadnought Class of powerful battleships of the early 20th century, named after a British ship.

factory ship A fishing vessel equipped with facilities for cleaning, filleting and freezing.

fire ship A vessel deliberately set on fire and left to drift among an enemy fleet, used in 16th-century warfare.

Galleon

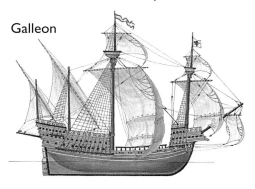

fore Towards the front of a ship.

forecastle Forward, raised part of a ship, often used for the crew's quarters.

frigate A term used at different times for several different types of vessels. In the 18th and 19th centuries, a frigate

Destroyer

carrack A large Mediterranean sailing ship, used for both cargo and warfare and popular with 15th-century explorers.

carvel The system of building wooden ships in which the planks are fixed together without overlapping.

catamaran A boat with twin hulls, which gives it extra stability.

corsair A pirate or privateer, especially from the Mediterranean or France.

destroyer Traditionally, a small, fast-moving battleship, although the term is now used for modern battleships of a range of sizes and functions.

dhow A lateen-sailed vessel used widely in the Arab world.

was a medium-sized sailing ship, with square sails. In modern Britain, a frigate is usually a warship smaller than a destroyer, while the United States' navy uses the term for a small escort ship.

galleon A large sailing ship, built high at fore and aft and used in warfare in the 15th and 16th centuries, especially by the Spanish.

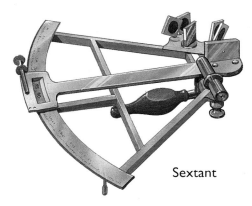

Sextant

galley A long ship, popular in the navies of the ancient world, powered by both oars and sails. It was developed by the Phoenicians.

hold The below-deck area of a ship, which is used to contain cargo.

ironclad A ship with a hull protected by iron plates. It was powered by steam engines.

Jolly Roger A pirate flag, usually consisting of a white skull and crossbones on a black background.

junk A flat-bottomed sailing ship of eastern Asia, rigged with square sails which are usually supported by thin wooden battens.

keel A ship's lowest timber, running the full length of the vessel from fore to aft and supporting the entire frame of the hull.

knot A unit of speed at sea – one nautical mile per hour. One knot is 1.852 kilometres an hour.

lateen The term used to describe a triangular sail.

Paddle steamer

latitude The distance from the equator. Lines of latitude run around the Earth, parallel with the equator.

liner A large passenger-carrying ship, run by a shipping company or line, usually offering luxury accommodation.

longitude The distance, measured in degrees, east or west of a line running through Greenwich, England. Lines of longitude run in great circles around the Earth, passing through the poles.

man of war A large sailing warship of the 18th and 19th centuries.

merchant ship A vessel used for carrying cargo.

oceanography The scientific study of the seas.

orlop deck The lowest deck on a ship, sometimes consisting of platforms laid over, or overlapping, beams in the hold.

pilot A seaman with detailed knowledge of their local coast, who helps guide ships into port.

privateer A person or ship authorized to rob or seize an enemy's ships.

propeller A shaft, formed in the shape of a spiral, turned by the engine to drive a ship.

rigging The network of ropes that helps hold up a ship's masts and allows her sails to be controlled.

rudder A large flat structure attached by hinges to the rear of a ship and turned to steer a vessel.

scurvy A disease of skin and gums caused by lack of vitamin C. It was discovered in the 18th century that eating plenty of fresh fruit and vegetables prevented this.

Tanker

sextant A navigational instrument used to measure the height of the Sun, enabling sailors to work out a ship's latitude.

stern The rear part of a vessel.

tanker A ship, usually large, that contains tanks to carry bulk liquids such as oil.

torpedo A self-propelled weapon, designed to travel under water, carrying an explosive charge that goes off when it hits its target.

trireme An ancient warship powered by three banks of oars on each side of the hull.

turbine engine An engine containing a wheel with vanes (rather like a waterwheel) which is pushed around by a fluid.

yard Crossbar, mounted at right-angles to a mast, which supports a sail.

Index

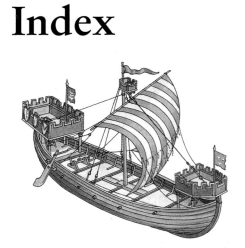

Acknowledgements

The publishers would like to thank the following
illustrators for their contributions to this book:

b = bottom, c = centre, l = left, r = right, t = top, m = middle

Susanna Addario 43 *tr*; **Marion Appleton** 44 *c*; **Mark Bergin** 1 *c*, 3 *l*, 36–37, 37 *t*, 38–39;
Harry Bishop 54 *b*, 55 *t*; **Peter Bull** 6–7; **Gino D'Achille** 21 *t*, 21 *cl*, 58–59; **Mike Davis** 35 *tl*, 38 *t*;
Peter Dennis 14–15, 16–17, 17 *tr*; **Ed Dovey** 40–41; **Richard Draper** 16 *b*; **Chris Forsey** 10 *tl*, 10 *cr*;
Christian Hook 17 *br*; **Roy Huxley** 37 *c*, 39 *tr*; **John James** 8–9, 13, 36 *tl*, 42; **Kevin Maddison** 8 *tr*, 11, 24–25,
46–47, 56 *t*; **Chris Molan** 20–21, 34–35, 45, 48–49; **Roger Payne** 54 *tl*; **Peter Ross** 44 *tr*; **Kevan Rush** 3 *t*, 22 *t*;
Rodney Shakell 45 *tl*; **Mike Taylor** 12 *tl*; **Thomas Trojer** 28–29.

The publishers would also like to thank the following
for supplying photographs for this book:

b = bottom, c = centre, l = left, r = right, t = top

Pages: **2** *br* The Bridgeman Art Library/Louvre, Paris, France; **3** *br* The Bridgeman Art Library/Bonhams, London;
4–5 Virgil Pomfret/Roger Desoutter; **10** *cl* Giraudon; **12** *tr* The Bridgeman Art Library/Metropolitan Museum
of Art, New York, USA; **14** *tl* Mary Evans Picture Library/Explorers Archives; **15** *tr* The Bridgeman Art Library/British
Library, London; **18** *bl* National Maritime Museum Picture Library; **18–19** Virgil Pomfret/Roger Desoutter; **19** *t* The
Bridgeman Art Library/Natural History Museum, London, *tl* The Art Archive/British Museum, *tr* The Art Archive;
22 *cr* Corbis/Bettmann, *bl* The Bridgeman Art Library/National Maritime Museum; **22–23** *c* Virgil Pomfret/Roger
Desoutter; **23** *tr* Corbis; **25** *tr* Kos Picture Source Ltd/David Williams; **26** *tr* U.S. Navy; **29** *b* The Bridgeman Art
Library/Musée de la Tapisserie, Bayeux, France; **30** *tr* The Mary Rose Trust, *b* AKG London/Archivio Cameraphoto
Venezia; **34** *tr* The Bridgeman Art Library/Private Collection, *c* The Art Archive/De Vries; **35** *tr* The Bridgeman Art
Library/Roderick Lovesey/David Messum Gallery, London (we have been unable to trace the copyright holder and
would be grateful to receive any information as to their identity); **38** *b* U.S. Navy; **43** *br* "Courtesy of the Pilgrim
Society, Plymouth, Massachusetts"/Bacon; **46** *tr* Corbis; **47** *tr* Science & Society Picture Library/Science Museum;
48 *tr* Peter Newark's Pictures; **49** *tr* Corbis/Bettmann, *cr* The Bridgeman Art Library/Victoria & Albert Museum,
London (we have been unable to trace the copyright holder and would be grateful to receive any information as to
their identity); **50** *cr* The Advertising Archive; *br* Science & Society Picture Library/National Railway Museum; **50–51** *t*
Princess Cruises; **51** *br* Virgil Pomfret/Roger Desoutter; **55** *br* Michael Holford; **56** *cl* Corbis; *c* Corbis; **57** *c* Corbis, *br*
National Maritime Museum Picture Library; **58** *tr* Corbis; **59** *t* Corbis, *c* The Art Archive/Dennis Cochrane Collection.

Every effort has been made to trace the copyright holders of the photographs.
The publishers apologise for any inconvenience caused.